FINANCIAL FREEDOM: "GENERATIONAL WEALTH" SEMINAR WORKBOOK

Edmund H. Moore, PhD
EHMOORE PEOPLE LLC
"Ever Helping More People"

Copyright:

All rights reserved. No part of this publication may be used either in print or electronic form without the written consent of Edmund H. Moore.
For information regarding personal appearances or interviews, please contact the O-Media Group, Olivia Almagro, at olivia.almagro@gmail.com

ISBN:

978-1-7373337-7-7
K.A.M.'s Publishing Co. LLC.
Los Angeles, CA 90008
www.kimamorrow.com

EHMOORE PEOPLE LLC
"Ever Helping More People"
8235 Old Troy Pike PMB 148
Huber Heights, Ohio 45424-1025
Edmundhmoore.com

DISCLAIMER STATEMENT:

This publication contains the opinions and ideas of the author based on life experiences. It is intended to provide helpful and useful information on the topics covered. It is sold with the intent that the author and publisher are not engaged in providing professional services through this book. Throughout this book, the author advises the reader or listener to seek professional advice from a competent professional.

The author and publisher specifically disclaim any responsibility for any liability, loss, or risk, personal or otherwise, which is incurred as a consequence, directly or indirectly, of the use and application of this book's contents.

THE AUTHOR

Edmund H. Moore, PhD, was formerly employed as a federal Department of Defense employee and is active in his community through his church, non-profit organizations (NPO), community boards, and volunteer efforts. Over the years, he has been involved with real estate, investment clubs, personal investing, and the like.

Edmund is a member of the Omega Psi Phi Fraternity, Inc., Sigma Xi, the American Ceramic Society, the NAACP, the Air Force Association, and many other affiliations. He has invested in or is invested in a few private equity startups.

Edmund received a PhD in Materials Science and Engineering from the University of Florida, Gainesville, FL; an MA in Management from Antioch McGregor, Yellow Springs, OH; and BS degrees in Physics and Mathematics from Florida A&M University, Tallahassee, FL. In addition, Dr. Moore received an SM in Materials Science and Engineering from the Massachusetts Institute of Technology, Cambridge, and an MA and an MS in Materials Science and Engineering from the University of Florida.

Dr. Moore has received several significant awards from the Air Force, fraternity, university, and others. He received the Florida A&M University National Alumni Association Distinguished Alumni Award—In the Field of Technology, an Air Force Award for Meritorious Civilian Service, and others.

He is the proud father of two daughters. He has authored several books, which include _With a Father's Love: 52 Weekly Letters to My Beloved Daughters._ In addition, he wrote a book titled _Village Wisdom for Our Youth,_ where all proceeds go to a Dayton, Ohio-based NPO, Parity Inc. Both books were published by Lift Bridge Publishing and are available on Amazon.com and through other vendors.

Table Of CONTENTS

01 | Introduction

03 | Session 1: Good Soil Required for Wealth

11 | Session 2: Financial Foundations

16 | Session 3: Know Your Numbers

21 | Session 4: Financial Streams & Opportunities

26 | Session 5: Protecting Your Assets

33 | Session 6: Planning

38 | Appendices: A, B, C.

45 | Thank You & Next Steps Toward Financial Freedom

INTRODUCTION

Every book that I write is based on my belief in Christ as my Lord and Savior. They are also written to focus on the community's good. A third quality of my books is that they should be easily readable by my family, community, and the average person at hopefully a fifth-grade level.

I have always had an interest in finances since my college days. I started an investment club with others in the 1980s, invested in Real Estate with friends, and started other business ventures with friends in the 1990s. My barrier was that I always seemed to be in college, then full-time employment, marriage, children, and aging parents who passed. Now, I am an empty nester.

My book on <u>Financial Freedom: *Doing Nothing is an Option*</u> was planned to be co-authored with one of my best friends. He passed before we could make much progress on the book; however, I included his experiences through his stories in the book that we shared along the journey. My late best friend, Mr. Richard R. Napier Sr., was a strong believer in Christ and one of the brightest people I ever met.

While neither of us is a licensed financial professional, our intent was to share our life experiences and "Best Practices" to help you get ahead in your life financially over time to place yourselves in a position to create financial freedom and, more importantly, generational wealth. Generational wealth, to be defined later, is important to position our families to help our churches and communities with our time, money, and other contributions.

Once the book was published and people found out about it, I was honored by my church, the Omega Baptist Church, 1821 Emerson Avenue, Dayton, Ohio 45406, to create a six-part seminar on Financial Freedom in 90-minute segments. I was overjoyed by the people who purchased the book, read it, and purchased the book for others. Many even shared with me things that they needed to do financially. Despite my schedule, I have taken up the challenge to share my nuggets on finances. My Audiobook should be ready in 2025, along with an updated Financial Freedom Workbook in 2025.

My purpose for this workbook is to guide you through the practices and principles necessary to achieve financial freedom. My hope is that this workbook imparts knowledge on life, the Word, and finances that help you and your families achieve financial freedom. Please note: one does not have to believe in Christ or other gods to achieve financial freedom or wealth. Wealth is generally achieved over decades, not over days. And remember, what you obtain too fast, you may not be able to retain.

The best way to use this workbook is to read the chapter summary and learn how to use the chapter material concepts to complete the exercises in each chapter. Once those concepts are learned, you will then apply them to your personal financial journey.

With that, let's get your journey started now!

SESSION #1
GOOD SOIL REQUIRED FOR WEALTH

The reference to **"Good Soil"** is a metaphor for you. How do you view finances (money)? How do you define wealth? Do you even believe in generational wealth or that it's possible? Have you examined your life to see why you are where you are in life (i.e., what are your behaviors that hinder you from achieving financial freedom)? How do you treat others, especially your family, i.e., practice the concept of forgiveness? And finally, who is part of your family?

The Bible has a story referred to as the **Parable of the Sower** that is found in Matthew 13:1-23 (NIV); the parable refers to the condition of the heart to receive the Word of God. The analogy to that scripture involves your actions as they relate to finances. Do you have a fixed or growth mindset? Are you able to learn from your failures? Are you able to acknowledge your fears and weaknesses? Are you willing to take any risk? And finally, are you willing to seek support from professionals versus free knowledge from your close acquaintances who may lack the knowledge or skill set in this area?

The biggest issue that most people have with finances (money) is a lack of money, being in debt, and not being able to get enough of it. That is our major antagonist as regards our feelings about money. How does one obtain, use, grow, and protect money?

The reason that we mostly have a lack of money is spiritual. It is due to a conflict with our flesh. Even our mind jumps into the fray, tormenting us about a lack of money. This lack of money is a constant war that we have with the flesh, as we always seek more.

The resolution of this conflict lies in our spirit. If we have a genuine spirit of love(like Christ), we can mostly overcome this battle of the flesh and mind. We can rely on Christ for our resources and be disciplined enough to secure a positive financial future. Because I am not a snake oil salesman, I posit (believe) that not everybody will achieve financial freedom in this world.

Let's look at some common definitions from your perspective before we dive into the course material further. (Seek to define your definitions using a maximum of 10-15 words.)

What is your view on finances?

_____
_____
_____

How do you define wealth?

_____
_____
_____

How do you define financial freedom?

_____
_____
_____

Can you define generational wealth? Is it possible?

_____
_____
_____

An interesting topic is who is in the **Middle Class**. A significant percentage of people in the United States of America (U.S.A.)—way over 50%—will say that they are members of the Middle Class. You can define the middle class by income, the number of family members, and geographical location in the U.S.A. It costs more to live in New York City, NY, than to live in Dayton, OH. The definition of the Middle Class differs in other countries.

I believe that the Middle Class should be defined by attributes (i.e., what you can do if you are a member of the Middle Class). The **Middle-Class attribute**s follow.

You are Middle Class if you:

- Own your home
- Can afford to educate your children
- Can take off and go on family vacations
- Can pay bills on time
- Have a secure source of income
- Can save and grow money

Those who believe in Christ realize that God provides for all our needs. It is God's favor that allows us to obtain wealth.

Wealth may also be defined by numbers: your cash value. Everyone has a different number. (Again, seek to define using a maximum of 10-15 words.)

How do you define wealth financially (cash value)?

_____
_____
_____

What does wealth consist of?

_____
_____
_____

Wealth may be defined by the following attributes and values:

- Attributes of wealth are cash, real estate, securities, royalties, family business ownership, children, and others
- Amounts: $100,000 ... $1,000,000 ... $5,000,000 ... $10M ... $50M ... $100M or more

Please note that there is a vast difference between being valued at $500,000 versus $2,000,000. This wealth is defined as one's net worth, not income. Why? One can earn $40M per year and spend $41M per year.

How does one define **Financial Freedom**? Financial freedom may simply be defined as the ability to pay off your family's living expenses forever without touching your core financial assets. This is true wealth, where you can just live off what your financial assets produce (passive income) without touching the principal (core assets).

What is your motivation for achieving financial freedom in 10-15 words?

_____
_____
_____

Next, we are addressing the topic of **Generational Wealth**. Families who exhibit this sort of wealth are the Dells, Hiltons, and Waltons. Just by looking at these names, you should be able to see the connection between the names and their industry.

How is Generational Wealth Defined?

- The ability to provide financially for your children and your children's children

- "A good man leaves an inheritance to his children's children" – Proverbs 13:22 (NKJV)

What are your motives for achieving generational wealth in 10-15 words?

_____
_____
_____

What are some barriers to achieving wealth? The following list is not inclusive of the barriers to achieving wealth.

Barriers to Achieving Wealth (a few)

- Medical debts
- Social injustices
- Poor health (physical, brain, and spiritual)
- Not paying your taxes
- Inadequate insurance coverage
- Overspending
- Inflation
- Poor reading and math skills
- Loaning money
- Divorces

As an exercise, write down your top three **financial vampires**, i.e., barriers to achieving wealth:

_____

_____

_____

This week's material started with the title of "Good Soil is Required for Wealth." A major issue with most of us is the condition of our hearts. Do we have the capacity to forgive others and not be judgmental? This is where the value of forgiveness comes into play.

The Value of Forgiveness

- Psychologists generally define forgiveness as a conscious, deliberate decision to release feelings of resentment or vengeance toward a person or group who has harmed you, regardless of whether they deserve your forgiveness.
- What does Christ say about forgiveness?
  ⇨ Mark 11:26
- How does that relate to family?
  ⇨ "Forgiveness does not change the past, but it does enlarge the future."
   – Paul Boese

Many other questions aforementioned fall into this arena of forgiveness: Do you have a fixed or growth mindset?

People who have a fixed mindset are less likely to forgive. They are less likely to learn from their own or others' failures. They tend to be people who do the same thing over and over based on their fixed mindset and are less likely to forgive others. Likewise, those with fixed mindsets are less likely to be able to acknowledge their/others' fears and weaknesses. They are also less willing to take any risk (i.e., please note that playing the lottery is not taking a risk—it is throwing away your money). Also, people with fixed mindsets are less willing to seek support from professionals versus free knowledge from close acquaintances. We need to have a growth mindset to grow in all areas. A growth mindset believes that there are enough resources in the world for everyone.

Finally, who is part of your family? You can gain financial freedom. But how do you pass along generational wealth if you have not defined your family and how it operates?

Define Your Family

- Do you have a Family Mission Statement
- Who is in your family (i.e., matriarch, patriarch, children, others)
- Who are we
- What are our values
- Family Purpose
- What is the role of the family
- How does the family view family wealth
- How does the family handle agreements and disagreements

Exercise: Define your family. You may eventually need to seek the assistance of professionals (financial and attorneys) to help with this process. (Please refer to my notes in Appendix C of my book).

In closing, when you are forgiving others, the easiest thing to tell someone in sincerity is, "I forgive you."

Likewise, when you have done someone wrong, the easiest way to express your remorse in sincerity is to say, "I am sorry."

Reference the book titled *Financial Freedom Book: Doing Nothing is an Option*, Chapters 1, 13, 15, and the Appendix for this section of the workbook.

SESSION #2
FINANCIAL FOUNDATIONS

Foundations are important for building wealth, creating wealth, and enhancing your faith walk. The Bible has a parable about building a house on sand that is found in Matthew 7:24-27 (NIV). The house built on a rock foundation withstood the storm, whereas the house built on sand failed. Thus, our finances need a solid **Financial Foundation.**

There are primarily three reasons for money: the **Purpose of Money**. The purpose of money is to either spend it, save it, invest it, or give it away. Way too often, it is common practice for us to blow money by not living within our means.

Proverbs 3:9-10 (NIV): Honor the Lord with your wealth...

My grandfather, Lee Moore Sr., had an imaginary smoking habit to save money. You, too, can adopt an imaginary practice or a mode to save money (e.g., save all your loose change, pay yourself first a set amount or percentage of your income by auto-deposit).

The **Spiritual Purposes of Money** are numerous. One may use money spiritually to serve the Lord's purposes.

Serve the Lord's Purposes

Deut. 8:18 (NIV): But remember the Lord your God, for it is He who gives you the ability to produce wealth, and so confirms His covenant, which He swore to your ancestors, as it is today.
Proverbs 3:9-10 (NIV): Honor the Lord with your wealth...your vats will brim over with new wine.

Take Care of Family

Discuss finances with your family. Expose the family to financial professionals. Live within your means.
Proverbs 2:2 (NIV): turning your ear to wisdom and applying your heart to understanding...

Invest in Opportunities
Invest to grow your financial resources.

Luke 16:11 (NIV): So, if you have not been trustworthy in handling worldly wealth, who will trust you with true riches?

Be Charitable
Deut. 15:11 (NIV): There will always be poor people in the land. Therefore, I command you to be openhanded toward your fellow Israelites who are poor and needy in your land.

Culturally, we tend to waste our financial resources due to a lack of family example and or self-education. Adequate financial education is not always provided in our families or the public education system. My philosophy on life involves God, family, finances and community—the F3C philosophy: Faith (in God), Family, Finances and Civics. There is always a debate on the order of the first two "F's" on whether God comes before the family or vice versa. Please note that you can't maintain the third "F" without civic engagement. Voting and civic engagement allow one to maintain their resources and community. Also, know your cultural and family history.

One must understand basic financial concepts as a foundation for achieving financial freedom. How does one define **Ownership and Net Worth**? Adequate reading skills (sixth grade) and basic math skills are required. Basic math skills include addition, subtraction, multiplication, division, fractions, percentages, and simple algebra. Know your basic math skills.

What are Financial Assets?

_____
_____
_____

What are non-financial assets?

_____
_____
_____

Financial assets include Cash Equivalents, Blockchain, and those held in retirement plans, health savings plans, education savings plans and others. **Non-financial assets** may include clothes, transportation, houses, jewelry, and others. There are **liquid assets** that can be readily converted to cash (e.g., savings accounts, money market accounts, etc.). **Illiquid assets** are difficult to rapidly convert to cash (e.g., a home, a boat, a car).

One thing that everyone can do is a **self-inventory of their assets**. (Refer to Appendix A.) An easy way to do that is to use a common computer software application like Excel or its equivalent to compile your assets. For clothes and household items, you can photograph them or videotape them for insurance purposes. A "Best Practice" is to retain your original receipts with the date of purchase and amount paid. Remember, you do not own an asset until it is fully paid off. If I owe $250 on my car, I do not own that car.

Also, ensure that your family members do a self-inventory of their assets. This should be done for any business venture that you own. Maintain good records, for if you become incapacitated or pass, your surviving family members may be in line to inherit your assets. Be sure that you pay attention to joint-owned property, partnerships, or private equity ventures.

Know your numbers as far as your assets are concerned, and even more for debt owed. There are typically three kinds of debt:

- Short-Term Debt (Pay off in a year: credit card)
- Medium-Term Debt (Pay off in 2-10 years: car payments)
- Long-Term Debt (Pay off in 15-30 years: home mortgage)

A great practice is to know your **net debt**. Your net debt may include:

- Personal: education loans, family loans, private loans
- Family: homes, other real property, credit cards
- Business: small business loans, micro-business loans, others

---

It is GOOD PRACTICE to use tax professionals or Certified Public Accountants (CPA) if you own a business venture, and even to do your personal taxes.

Now that you know your assets and debts, you can determine your net worth. Your Net Worth is defined as:

Net Worth (NW) = Assets (A) − Debts (D)

If the number is positive, you are liquid, and if the number is negative, you are illiquid (in debt).

Historically to the present: There is a Significant Wealth Gap in the U.S. According to the Brookings Institution, the median white household has a net worth of $188,200. That is about eight times more than a Black household of $24,100.

What are you going to do about it? We know about redlining, the Tulsa race riots, higher interest payments, and more that affect African American and low-income communities.

Now we are getting to a true foundation principle: **Budgets.** Budgets define your priorities. Where you spend or allocate your resources defines what you value. Based on Maslow's Hierarchy, we have three basic needs (food, water, and shelter). I believe that NASA added a couple of others in air and sleep. Now, another true need is a smartphone.

Levels two through five of Maslow's Hierarchy are:

- Physical safety (2)
- Love and belonging (3)
- Self-esteem (4)
- Self-fulfillment (5)

EXERCISE for Next Week (see Appendix B of the book):
- Track Your Spending This Week and Prepare a Budget
- If you have the data, prepare a budget for one, three, six, or twelve months

Maintain Relevant Documents

- Bank, Credit Union, Fintech accounts
- Brokerage accounts (taxable and retirement)
- 401(k), Thrift Savings Plan, and another equivalent
- Bonds
- Private Equity contracts
- Personal loan agreements
- Recurring bills and outstanding debts
- Home mortgage or ownership paperwork
- Auto loan or ownership paperwork
- Insurance policies
- Social Security and other annuity benefit records
- Tax records for five years (indefinitely for homes)
- Estate planning documents (trusts, wills, etc.)

To close, ensure you retain maintenance and improvement records for homes/properties. And one should always strive to have short and long-term goals.

Reference the book titled *Financial Freedom: Doing Nothing is an Option*, Chapters 2 through 7, for this session in the workbook.

Bonus Exercise: Use this personal financial statement (PFS) link to tally your assets:

https://www.regions.com/virtualDocuments/Financial_Statement.pdf

SESSION #3
KNOW YOUR NUMBERS

Now, let's delve deeper into the Dirty B-Word (Budgets) further. The best way to put together a budget is:
- Track your daily costs for three months
- Adjust for any missed bills payable every six months or once per year
- Include an emergency ("Rainy Day") fund to manage risks
- Adjust your budget as things change (anticipate)

TABLE 1: Budget Illustration and Allocation Exercise (End of Year Annual Expenses)

CATEGORIES	PROJECTED	ACTUAL	DIFFERENCE
SHELTER	-	-	-
TRANSPORTATION	-	-	-
SAVINGS	$20,000	$18,000	($2,000)
CHARITABLE	-	-	-
FOOD	$4,800	$5,500	($700)
INSURANCE	-	-	-
CLOTHING	-	-	-
UTILITIES	$1,800	$1,200	$600

In Table 1, the expenses came in $2,100 less than expected, and resulted in a food bill $700 too high. The savings in the utility bill were $600. However, the savings goal was unmet.

TABLE 2: Budget Illustration and Allocation Exercise
(End of Year Annual Income)

CATEGORIES	PROJECTED	ACTUAL	DIFFERENCE
SALARY	$40,000	$40,000	$0.00
PARTNER SALARY	$32,000	$34,000	$2,000
RENTAL	$5,000	$2,500	($2,500)
OTHER	$3,000	$1,500	($1,500)

In Table Two, the income came in $2,000 short of what was expected. Income projections were higher for the partner's salary. However, the rental and other income was short by $4,000. That was ameliorated by not saving $2,000 which allowed a balanced budget with a $100 surplus.

There are a variety of categories or descriptions to define budget allocations. They include auto, business, charity, clothes, dependent care, education, entertainment, food, home, insurance, medical/dental, savings/investments, taxes, utilities, travel, fraternal/sorority, etc.

Refer to Appendix B of _Financial Freedom: Doing Nothing is an Option_ for sample budget categories.

Proverbs 21:5 (NIV): The plans of the diligent lead to profit as surely as haste leads to poverty.

Budget allocation: "Best Practices" or examples are numerous. Some suggest 10% (God): 35% (Housing): 15% (Save): 40% (Live). Another ratio is 50% (Needs): 30% (Wants): 20% (Save). There is no one right universal allocation for budgets. However, be sure to have a Rainy Day Fund, also known as (aka) a Holy Sh_t Fund to cover emergencies. Visit the very helpful "Budgeting Calculator" at TheBalanceMoney.com site.

The **Rainy Day Fund** should cover your expenses if you face a traumatic event such as a loss of job or employment, a relative who needs a bond, or some other emergency.

Many financial professionals recommend Rainy Day funds for six to twelve months. However, it should fit your circumstances. You may need up to twenty-four months. I was told by a colleague that she was taught to have a fifteen-month emergency fund (i.e., a year to live and three months to live when finding a new job). Your rainy day funds should be liquid. **Note:** Avoid Pay Day loans, which are high-interest loans, and Bill Me Now Pay Later loans for emergencies. *Bankrate.com* revealed in 2022 that four in ten Americans did not have enough savings to cover an unplanned (emergency) expense of $1,000.

The concept of Cash Flow is simple: It tracks money in and money out. You are good if your balance is always positive, i.e., cash in should be greater than cash out.

In Chapters 9 and 10, the concept of **Debt** was discussed. Bad debt and good debt are discussed. Your payment of debt should be a category in your budget.

Proverbs 22:7 (NIV): The rich rule over the poor, and the borrower is a slave to the lender.

What are some examples of bad debt?

_____
_____
_____

What are some examples of good debt?

_____
_____
_____

Debt Payoff Strategies were discussed in the book. Three of these strategies follow, i.e., pay your debt as follows:

- High Interest First
- Lowest Amount First
- Always Pay Your Taxes First

What is the benefit of paying your bills on time?

_____
_____
_____

When you pay your bills on time, you can establish good credit and sleep better at night.

Credit is discussed in Chapter 11. Credit is essentially the balance in a person's favor in an account. The concept of Debt Load is discussed there as well. In 10 to 15 words, define the following concepts.

What is the definition of debt load?

_____
_____
_____

How does one establish good credit?

_____
_____
_____

What is the importance of credit?

_____
_____
_____

One of my daughters recently asked me what factors make up good credit. I asked her if she had read my book. Nonetheless, there are five weighted factors that are used to establish good credit with your Fair, Isaac and Company (FICO) score, as follows:

- 35% Payment History
- 30% Amounts Owed
- 15% Length of Credit History
- 10% New Credit
- 10% Credit Mix

Know the importance of credit. It allows you to borrow other people's money at a lower rate of interest over time. Be sure to know how your payment history and credit mix affect your credit rating. What does declaring bankruptcy do for your credit?

Best Practice: Carry at least two credit cards that you pay in full monthly. Obtain rewards points that you can use when feasible. In many cases, they offer insurance protection and the power to dispute purchases. You don't have to carry cash. Personally, I do not like debit cards. However, one can autopay their bills with their debit card to automatically balance their financial statement. The debit cards allow one to cyber-securely pay bills through their financial institution via bill pay. My issue with debit cards is that the payment comes out of my account automatically and offers less power to dispute transactions.

Debt load is a measure of your income-to-debt ratio or your assets-to-debt ratio.

Reference the book titled *Financial Freedom: Doing Nothing is an Option*, Chapters 7 through 11 for this session.

SESSION #4
FINANCIAL STREAMS & OPPORTUNITIES

This session will cover the eight streams of income that are sometimes reduced to seven. One may define **income** as money that is regularly received through work, investments, or other means. The average millionaire has at least six streams of income.

The eight streams of income found in Chapter 12 of the book are:

- Earned income as an employee
- Profit income earned from buying and selling products
- Interest income earned from loaning money
- Dividend income from owning company equity
- Rental income from renting out properties
- Capital gains income from the sale of appreciated assets
- Royalty income
- Residual income earned when a job is done, and you still get paid

I believe that residual income is ill-defined and is duplicative across the other streams of income. I would eliminate it as a category and go with seven streams of income.

Ecclesiastes 11:2 (NIV): Invest in seven ventures, yes in eight; you do not know what disaster may come upon the land.

What is an example of Royalty income?

_____
_____
_____

In many communities that lack amenities, they suffer from being **unbanked** versus being **banked** in too many instances. Unbanked means that one is not involved in a financial institution like a bank or credit union. They operate on a cash basis. One cannot legally build financial wealth without being part of the financial system. Of course, banking means that you have accounts in a financial institution and use some of its additional services.

If you are unbanked, your money is probably stored under your bed, in a shoebox, in a post office box, in a safe, or some other hiding place. That money is not invested and is not growing; in reality, its value is being consumed (diminished) by inflation.

When I was a Boy Scout, we were advised for health reasons to drink from moving streams of water versus consuming stagnant bodies of water. Stagnant (scared) money does not make money. Nothing grows in stagnant ponds.

As an investor, time is our greatest ally. The time invested provides an opportunity for appreciation (growth). That is where the **Rule of 72** comes into play.

How does the Rule of 72 work?

- Divide 72 by your annual rate of return to calculate the years it would take to double your money

- For example, $500 would double to $1,000 in 12 years at a 6% annual rate of return

---

To reiterate, a key to creating wealth is time (years) invested. A middle-class person can create wealth. The example in the African American communities prior to school integration was schoolteachers who worked for forty years and paid into their pensions, and saved their money. Many became millionaires.

An easier route to attaining **generational wealth** is to be a **High-Income professional**. Refer to Chapter 18 of the book. There are degrees that lead to high earned incomes for many people, as follows:

- Doctor
- Investment Banker
- Petroleum Engineer
- Data Scientist
- R&D Manager
- Surgeon
- Corporate Executive
- Corporate Executive
- Lawyer
- Dentist

One attribute that many of the above professions have is that they require college degrees. In the past, one could become a corporate executive without a degree, but those days have mostly passed. Please note that there are many other jobs that make far more earned income, but are not readily achievable by the masses. Examples include salespeople, engineers, and nurses. The trades allow for high incomes as well: plumbers, electricians, and others.

The government and the Internal Revenue Service (IRS) have set up savings vehicles that allow one to save and invest money. These savings vehicles allow for tax breaks on a variety of other investment vehicles. (Refer to Chapters 12 and 14 of the book for more information in these areas.)

Many families have used **Life Insurance** as a vehicle to create financial freedom and generational wealth. Uncle Clyde may have a $1M life insurance policy that, upon his death, creates wealth for his surviving family members. Upon his death by natural causes, i.e., not by suicide or another uncovered means, Clyde's family will be enriched.

Many people purchase **homes** that appreciate (increase) in value and that value is often used for **Home Equity Lines of Credit** (HELOC) to build wealth. Homes can, in turn, be left for future generations. Real Estate: homes, land, commercial property, and other real assets fall under this category.

Not being tied down with debt for higher education allows one to achieve financial freedom. The use of **Educational Savings Plans** (529 Plans) allows for one's future generations to graduate from higher education with no debt or minimal debt. Life is so much sweeter without debt.

Your health is important to achieving financial freedom. Life is tough when one endures chronic health conditions. You can save money using **Health Savings Accounts** (HSAs).

Next, we will discuss more common savings and investment options, found in Chapter 14.

Some basic saving options include:

- Simple Savings Account
- Treasury Inflation-Protected Security (TIPS)
- Certificate of Deposit (CD)
- Money Market Account (MMA)

Exercise: Be sure to look up what TIPS are.

What are TIPS?

_____
_____
_____

What is the difference between a simple savings account and an MMA?

_____
_____
_____

Do CDs offer more upside (higher interest returns) than MMAs?

_____
_____
_____

The more traditional tax savings investment options follow. If you are employed and a company offers you one of these tax savings investment options with a match, please contribute enough in your plan to meet the employee match (i.e., free money).

The Tax Savings Investment Options follow:

- Traditional Individual Retirement Account (IRA)
- ROTH IRA
- 401(k) or Thrift Savings Plan (TSP) or equivalent
- Simplified Employee Pension (SEP)
- Health Savings Account (HSA)
- Educational Savings Plan (529 Plans)
- Others

Real Estate investment has been mentioned prior: Residential, Commercial, and Other. Real Estate Investment Trust (REIT) falls into this arena, versus having to own real property. Research REITs.

Be very careful with blockchain investments. Be sure that you understand any investment, and be careful if the returns are too good. For example, you can invest in opportunities around blockchains that allow that technology to be executed. For example, I invested in NVIDIA, a company that produced the technology that allowed the mining of Bitcoins.

NOTE: Consider the importance of volatility in all your investment decisions. Another term for this is risk tolerance. How much risk to your investment returns are you willing to stomach?

What is volatility?

_____
_____
_____

SESSION #5
PROTECTING YOUR ASSETS

Once you have acquired and even as you are acquiring assets, you still must protect them. The topic of Asset Protection is found in Chapter 16 of the book. The Bible alludes to wealth protection in Matthew 25:14 (NIV): *Again, it will be like a man going on a journey, who called his servants and entrusted his wealth to them.*

One of the primary tools for protecting your assets is insurance. There are numerous types of insurance. Some of the more common types of insurance are:

- Life Insurance (Whole, Universal, Variable Universal)
- Term Life Insurance
- Home/Property Insurance
- Health Insurance
- Disability Insurance
- Property Insurance
- Liability Insurance
- Personal Umbrella Insurance
- Long-term Care Insurance
- Many others: insure your hand, artwork, boats, cyber

One of the common things that we observe far too often is a family that does not have the funds to bury a loved one. After completing this section, one should not find oneself in that position.

What type of insurance can one obtain to pay for their burial expenses?

_____
_____
_____

What is an alternate mode to paying for one's burial expenses?

_____
_____
_____

Visit a site like *policygenius.com* to review various types of insurance products or visit an insurance professional.

Review your insurance products and determine if you need disability insurance based on your age and life circumstances. Most of those who have residences (home or rental) have insurance to cover their property. And if you own a home, home insurance is needed. Please note that in some states, FL and CA, the cost of home insurance is so expensive that many homeowners self-insure or go without home insurance. The insurance that you have on your life can vary based on your circumstances. I have long-term care (LTC) insurance as a single parent.

A very important step is to do **Estate Planning**. The easiest thing that everyone over eighteen years of age should do is to do their first **Will**. When you turn eighteen, I recommend that you register to vote and prepare your Will. Many well-known celebrities have passed without a Will, and that has caused their loved ones considerable pain and agony when closing out their estates.

What celebrities have you recently heard of that had no Will on their death? And what problems did their family endure?
_____
_____
_____

As you are preparing your Will that informs your loved ones of what you wish to do with your personal property, assets, burial (end-of-life) plans, and other matters, don't forget about **Power of Attorney** (POA) documents. When you become incapacitated (a fancy word for you not being able to voice your views due to an illness or other malady), you need someone to be able to communicate your health wishes and handle your finances. A Medical or Health POA allows one to speak on your behalf to the healthcare providers. A Financial POA allows one to handle your finances (pay bills and do other financial transactions). Keep those POAs updated.

A **Trust** is a very useful legal instrument. It is like a bowl for you to place your Wills, POAs, assets, and other documentation into one place. In certain cases, a Trust is just as effective as a prenuptial agreement. There are two types of Trusts, as follows:

- Revocable
- Irrevocable

What is the difference between a revocable and an irrevocable Trust?
_____
_____
_____

> While you are building your assets and setting a solid foundation for your finances, most of you will need a team to assist you. Many of you will require the following professionals:
>
> - Banker, Credit, Union, Online Financial Institution
> - Investment Advisor and Certified Financial Planner
> - Insurance Broker or Professional
> - Certified Public Accountant (CPA) or Tax Preparer/Professional
> - Various Attorneys (Trust, Will, Property, Business, etc.)
> - Realtors
> - Funeral Home
> - Charitable Foundations
> - Other

If I am making my money from property rentals, I need all the professionals that are required to maintain my property. Those include property management, plumbers, electricians, roofers, and handymen. This is in addition to an attorney, insurance, and a financial professional.

I encourage you to build a team of qualified, honest, and reputable professionals to help you grow your finances and provide you with the tax-efficient strategies to transfer your wealth to future generations. I make charitable donations through my church, the Combined Federal Campaign (CFC), The Dayton Foundation (TDF), and through individual donations to numerous causes.

Now, returning to owning and operating a business. Seek the right professionals and community organizations to help you with deciding on what business entity is right for you. Should it operate as?

> - Sole Owner
> - Limited Liability Corporation (LLC)
> - Partnership
> - Corporation

Should your business be for-profit or a non-profit? You really need to consult appropriate professionals to help you make the right decision on how your business is operated.

Document Your Life – the Documenting Your Life Chapter is found at the end of the book titled _Financial Freedom: Doing Nothing is an Option._

Financial Accounts: Banking (savings, money market accounts), TIPS, equity (stocks, ETFs), bonds, mutual funds, cryptocurrency, etc.

Insurance Policies: life, home, auto, umbrella, disability, flood, riders, long-term care, other

Business Records: assets, inventory, debts, taxes, other

Material Possessions: homes, rental properties, vehicles, boats, airplanes, farm equipment, jewelry, and more

Miscellaneous: Last five years of tax records, debts, and other

Organizing your life falls under three categories.

A Filing System:
Store documents securely by paper, electronically, or both. Use a fireproof filing cabinet, cloud storage online, or electronic storage devices in multiple physical locations. Update every six months or when major life events occur.

Emergency Items and Contacts:

Keep updating mailing addresses, email, and phone numbers for emergency contacts (e.g., executors, investment or financial professionals, attorneys, insurance agents, accountants, CPAs, tax preparers, supervisors, medical professionals to include dentists and doctors, home health aides, family members, and more).

Documents required upon serious injury or death include:

- Copy of health care proxy (Living Will)
- Durable power of attorney (Financial and Medical)
- Financial institutions' Power of Attorney forms completed (maybe proprietary)
- Obituary information (resume or bio)
- Donation preference to family, friends, and charities
- Location of safe with access (keys or combination)
- Passport/Citizenship (naturalization papers)
- List of online accounts and passwords
- Burial instructions, funeral home and burial plot deed
- Passport/Citizenship (naturalization papers)
- Birth Certificate (Death Certificate for the deceased)
- Phone number and address of County Surrogate for Orphans or Orphan's Court (to probate a Will)
- Trust
- Discharge papers for military
- Certified copy of Last Will and Testament
- Instruction letter for the executor
- Safety deposit box keys

Documents for Financial and Health Insurance and Other Items

- Tax documents
- Investment and assets management
- Banks, credit unions, fintech, mortgages, and loans
- Mutual funds and equities
- Retirement and pension plans
- Other corporate benefits
- Health insurance
- Life insurance and long-term care insurance
- Property and casualty insurance
- Annuities to include social security
- Trusts and other financial plans
- Titles and deeds
- Credit cards
- Other legal documents
- Telephone and cell phones
- Utilities
- Warranties, service contracts, and instructions

Items for the recently deceased are the following:

- Last Will and Testament
- Military Discharge papers, if applicable
- Burial instructions
- Cemetery plot deed, prepaid cremation documents
- Funeral home preference and information
- Charitable donations, if applicable
- A letter of instruction
- Death Certificate (order at least 10)
- Information for the obituary
- The phone number of your County Surrogate Court (i.e., the county clerk or clerk's Office to probate the Last Will and Testament by the executor)

The executor should obtain enough death certificates to transfer the ownership of all accounts and titles of ownership for the deceased. One or two may be sufficient for a deceased person with little to no assets.

Emergency Information:

Ready Accessible Documents
- Social Security Card
- Birth Certificate
- Passport or Naturalization Papers
- Driver's License number (with expiration date)
- Marriage Certificate
- Divorce or Separation Papers
- Prenuptial Agreements
- Adoption Papers
- Safe and Safe Deposit Box Keys and/or Combinations

Broad Categories of Emergency Papers/Information:

Emergency Documents to Settle Claims

Investment Documents (transfer ownership)

- ◆ Per Credit Applications
- ◆ Per Last Will and Testament

Insurance and Annuity Documents (to settle claims)

Bank and Credit Documents

- ◆ Access to Cash to Settle Estate Affairs
- ◆ Documents to Settle Outstanding Credit Accounts

Personal Finance Documents

- ◆ Transfer Ownership Per Last Will and Testament
- ◆ Documents Needed to Settle Debts

Items for the Seriously Ill

- ◆ Living Will and Health Care Proxy
- ◆ Durable Power of Attorney (POA)
- ◆ Financial Institution's Proprietary POA

Items for the Recently Deceased

SESSION #6

PLANNING

We have now hit the last session. This will be a combination of a review of the professionals you need to help achieve financial freedom and grow your wealth (refer to Chapter 19 of the book).

Next, what is your thought process for compiling a plan to generate and transfer wealth? Unless you have an incurable disease and plan to pass before you reach retirement age, you must plan for retirement. Be aware that many have a plan to work until they die as their retirement plan. Plan on how you will reach a number that allows you to retire. If you are fortunate, you can live off passive versus earned income during retirement. Before you retire, plan on doing a self-stress test to see if your plan is sound.

One of the things I highlighted to my daughters at a very young age was that the best athletes in the world all tend to use professional trainers. Tiger Woods and Tom Brady each have a coach. Chief Executive Officers (CEOs) have certified life coaches and personal consultants to improve their performance. I recently heard Clark Atlanta's Dr. Daniel Black remark, "The job of the coach is to move you past your ego." Don't let your ego be a barrier to your financial success.

Be sure to use a team of coaches (Professionals)

- Certified Public Accountants (CPAs)
- Others: Property Managers, Plumbers, Electricians, etc.
- Realtors and Real Estate Attorneys
- Certified Financial Planners
- Professional Tax Preparers
- Various Attorneys (Trust, Estate, Business, etc.)
- Investment Managers
- Insurance Professionals

NOTE: Build a team and don't try to do everything yourself. A caterer once told me that he could make more money with good help than trying to do everything himself.

> Have a **plan for generating wealth** (refer to Chapter 21 of the book). My generic roadmap to generational wealth follows:
> - God is my source
> - First provisions go to God at 10% or more
> - Live within my means and have a budget
> - Records are a must
> - Spend wisely and put aside (encumber, save) funds
> - Be content with God's provisions (but not lazy)
> - Invest to grow your wealth (legal financial system)
> - Place appropriate professionals on your team
> - Build a family culture of life-long financial learning
> - Make it fun
> - Different strategies are required for different levels

Nothing in my plan above talked about money or plans to generate financial freedom or wealth. Essentially, my plan was to work until I was fifty-five; live within my means; save and invest 10% to 15% of my gross income; rely on the Rule of 72 to generate a minimum of 6% annual return; own my house and have no debt by the age of fifty-five; contribute to my church and to charities; invest in various opportunities; educate my family and self on civics/history/finances; take care of my family and enjoy life. Hopefully place yourself in a position to protect your family and transfer generational wealth to the next two generations (children and grandchildren).

When I say different strategies are required for different levels, I mean it takes different financial strategies to manage $50,000 versus $500,000 versus $2 million versus $25 million, or even $100 million or more. If you have not educated yourself on finances, you can't hold onto the money—that is why many lottery winners and athletes end up broke. Again, it takes different strategies to manage $500,000 versus $25 million. You may need more professionals to help you manage the $25 million and take advantage of more tax-savings strategies that are not available to you with $500,000.

What is my retirement plan?

One saying that has never been wrong is, "It does not matter how much you earn; it matters how much you save and invest." I can have more wealth by earning $25,000 per year than someone earning $1 million per year. The lesson: don't spend more than you earn.

Retirement is found in Chapter 17 of the book. There are three steps: know your number, know how to reach your number, and know your financial sources for your retirement.

Know Your Number (i.e., what is my number)?
- How much do you need to retire by a certain age (e.g., $500,000 at age 65)
- Do you know your sources of income (i.e., pension, annuity, savings, others)
- Do you know the cost of your healthcare

How Do You Reach Your Number?
- Save and invest over time using the Rule of 72
- Sell a business or intellectual property
- Rental income
- Remember the seven streams of income

Can You Finance Your Retirement?
- Is my passive income sufficient
- Do I require earned income

The **Self Stress Test** is covered in Chapter 20. Many people have become homeless via natural disasters. The following is not an exhaustive list of scenarios that you should be able to overcome or be prepared to handle:

- Do you have a sufficient nest egg
- Can you survive a divorce
- Can you survive disability
- Are you prepared for reasonable unplanned expenses
- Is your plan communicated and sustainable
- Have you done an estate plan checkup
- Are your critical records accessible to your family upon your incapacity

Closing Remarks

Most people and families do nothing to plan for financial freedom. There is no generational wealth without financial freedom. Train yourself on finances and ensure your family is trained.

"If you wish to be successful in life, get off your butt and get started." – Edmund H. Moore, PhD.

"When you turn eighteen years of age in America, register to vote and prepare your first Will." – Edmund H. Moore, PhD

Appendices A, B, & C

Appendix A

Sample Estate Inventory

(While Living) When making an inventory of your estate, include the type of assets that your executor would seek. Based on your financial situation, your personal estate inventory may include:

- A 401(k) plan or similar employer-sponsored retirement plan
- One or more IRAs
- Business retirement accounts, such as a solo 401(k) or SEP IRA if you are self-employed
- One or more taxable brokerage accounts
- A Health Savings Account (HSA)
- College savings accounts
- Life insurance or disability insurance
- Bank accounts
- Vehicles you own
- Real estate and land that you own
- Personal possessions that you estimate are valued at $500 or more
- Family heirlooms, antiques and collectibles

Your spouse and you may want to create an estate inventory showing assets jointly owned and separately owned as individuals. Note that the assets acquired after marriage are owned by both spouses if you live in a community property state.

Sample Estate Inventory

(After Death) An estate inventory includes all assets of an estate belonging to someone who has passed away. This inventory can include a listing of the deceased person's liabilities or debts.

Here's what's included in an estate inventory on the liabilities side:

- First and second mortgage loans associated with any real estate included in assets
- Outstanding personal loans
- Private student loans
- Vehicle loans associated with a vehicle included on the asset side of the inventory
- Credit cards and open lines of credit
- Business loans
- Unpaid medical bills
- Unpaid taxes
- Any other outstanding debts, including unpaid court judgments

In terms of assets, items that would need to be added to an estate inventory include:

- Bank accounts, including checking accounts, savings accounts, money market accounts and CDs
- Personal investment accounts, including brokerage accounts, margin accounts, individual retirement accounts (IRAs), health savings accounts (HSAs), and college savings accounts
- Business interests, including partnerships, corporations, limited liability companies (LLCs), and sole proprietorships
- Real estate, including personal residences and investment properties
- Pension plans and workplace retirement accounts, such as 401(k)s, 403(b)s and 457 plans
- Insurance policies, including life insurance, disability insurance, annuities and long-term care insurance
- Intellectual property, such as copyrights, trademarks and patents
- Household items
- Personal effects, which can include heirlooms, antiques and collectibles
- Vehicles

Reference:
https://www.yahoo.com/lifestyle/included-estate-inventory-194615735.html

Appendix B

Sample Estate Inventory

Sample Budget (Visit the following Budget Tool):
https://files.consumerfinance.gov/f/documents/cfpb_well-being_monthly-budget.pdf

This tool allows one to use monthly income and expenses to prepare a **monthly budget.**

1. List of your income
2. List your expenses
3. Subtract your total spending from your total income to build a budget

Types of Income (amount gained) – add the totals for each month:

- Job
- Government Program
- Bank accounts
- Disability Benefits
- Financial Support
- Other Income

Type of Spending (amount spent) – add the totals for each month

- Housing (rent or mortgage)
- Utilities gas, water, sewage, electricity)
- Groceries plus other supplies
- Health expenses
- Transportation
- Education plus childcare
- Internet plus cable
- Pets plus service animals
- Savings and investments
- Cell phone
- Clothing
- Elder care
- Debt payments
- Other

Build Your Monthly Balanced Budget:

Total monthly income – Total monthly spending = 0.00

Note:

If your income is more than your expenses, you can save or spend that money.

If your expenses exceed your income, you must cut budget expenses or increase income.

Again, an excellent budgeting tool can be found at TheBalanceMoney.com site under the "Budgeting Calculator."

Appendix C

Family Mission Statement

Sample Family Mission Statement (Reference: 2021 Morgan Stanley Smith Barney LLC, Member SIPC; CRC 3453309 02/21 CS 9987351 03/21);

The Reference link follows:
https://advisor.morganstanley.com/michelle.ward/documents/field/m/mi/michelle-ward/WM%20Sample%20Family%20Mission%20Statement.pdf

Highlights for the Sample of a Family Mission Statement follow:
Statement of Mission of the MATRIARCH, PATRIARCH and CHILDREN families.

Purpose
The Statement of Mission is intended to express the values, philosophy, vision and mission of the BLANK Family, referred to in this document as the "Family". For simplicity, we refer to this document as our Statement of Mission. It reflects the participation of several generations of the Family from descendants through current family, and … FILL IN THE REST.

Who Are We?
We believe that our special identity as a Family begins with our descendants and who we identify as our patriarch and matriarch. Numbering them as our first, there are now four generations of the Family and three living members, as of today. While we identify ourselves as one Family, as the title of this document makes clear, we have different branches. We recognize that each branch has brought different and valuable energy, purpose, and vitality to the Family. FILL IN THE REST.

Our Values
We believe that our shared values are the essence of our Family identity. The sum of our values is our most singular and important distinguishing characteristic of our Family. As a Family, we:
- Honor the primacy of Family;
- Respect and encourage individual achievement and self-actualization;
- FILL IN THE REST

We believe our Family name is, in some sense, our most important asset. FILL IN THE REST.

The Role of the Family

We believe the Family should:
- Be a haven, yet not an island;
- Be close, yet not confining;
- FILL IN THE REST

The Family is one of the structures within which each of us lives. It gives us the guidance we need to grow, the freedom we need to establish our separate identity, and the support we need to confront challenges.

There are other structures, as well, within which we live, and the Family helps us to define our place within those structures. FILL IN THE REST.

Family Wealth

The Company, established by our patriarch and the legacies they have provided, has given the Family a measurable degree of economic wealth. The individual efforts of the descendants of BLANK, and the leadership of Some Financial Entity, our Family Office, have helped to preserve and increase the economic wealth. FILL IN THE REST

Family Accord and Discord

This document is tangible proof that there is much that we agree on as a Family. We hope that this is always the case, as it is now, that our agreements significantly outnumber our disagreements, especially on matters that are central to our Family identity. Nevertheless, we recognize that there will be disagreements and perhaps even discord within the Family. To that end, we commit:

- To strive to be respectful to one another;
- To encourage full participation in Family matters, taking into account individual maturity and responsibility;
- FILL IN THE REST

We sign the Mission Statement freely and enthusiastically this ___ day of ____. reference the above link to see the full sample Family Mission Statement. And visit a financial professional with estate planning expertise for assistance.

THANK YOU & NEXT STEPS TOWARD FINANCIAL FREEDOM

From the Desk of Dr. Edmund H. Moore

Dear Reader,

Thank you for investing your time, energy, and faith in *Financial Freedom: Doing Nothing is an Option.*

What You Can Do Next:
- **Live the Mission:** Apply the principles from each session—budgeting, asset protection, planning, and forgiveness—in your daily life.
- **Build Your Team:** Surround yourself with trusted financial, legal, and spiritual advisors.
- **Teach the Next Generation:** Share what you've learned. Financial literacy is one of the greatest gifts we can pass on.
- **Join Our Community:** Stay connected for upcoming seminars, the Financial Freedom Audiobook, and the 2025 edition of this workbook. The 2nd edition of my book is done and ready for purchase—it will be sold under the same title.

Leave a Review, Inspire Others
If this workbook made a difference in your life, please take a moment to leave a review. Your feedback helps others discover this resource and begin their own journey to financial freedom.

Leave your review on Amazon or your preferred bookseller site.

Your voice matters—and it may be just what someone else needs to get started.

"If you wish to be successful in life, get off your butt and get started."
– Dr. Edmund H. Moore

LET'S STAY CONNECTED

- **Visit My Website:** www.edmundhmoore.com
- **Contact for Speaking or Workshops:** olivia.almagro@gmail.com
- **Published by**: K.A.M.'s Publishing Co. LLC | www.kimamorrow.com

Ready to go deeper? Invite Dr. Moore to speak at your church, school, or community group.

Want to help others get started? Purchase bulk copies of the workbook for your family, ministry, or nonprofit.

This is your moment. Your future self—and your future generations—are counting on you.

www.ingramcontent.com/pod-product-compliance
Lightning Source LLC
Chambersburg PA
CBHW061122070526
44583CB00028B/3359